I just ate my friend

Heidi McKinnon

ALLEN & UNWIN

SYDNEY · MELBOURNE · AUCKLAND · LONDON

I just ate my friend.

He was a good friend,
but now he's gone.

Hello! Would you be my friend?

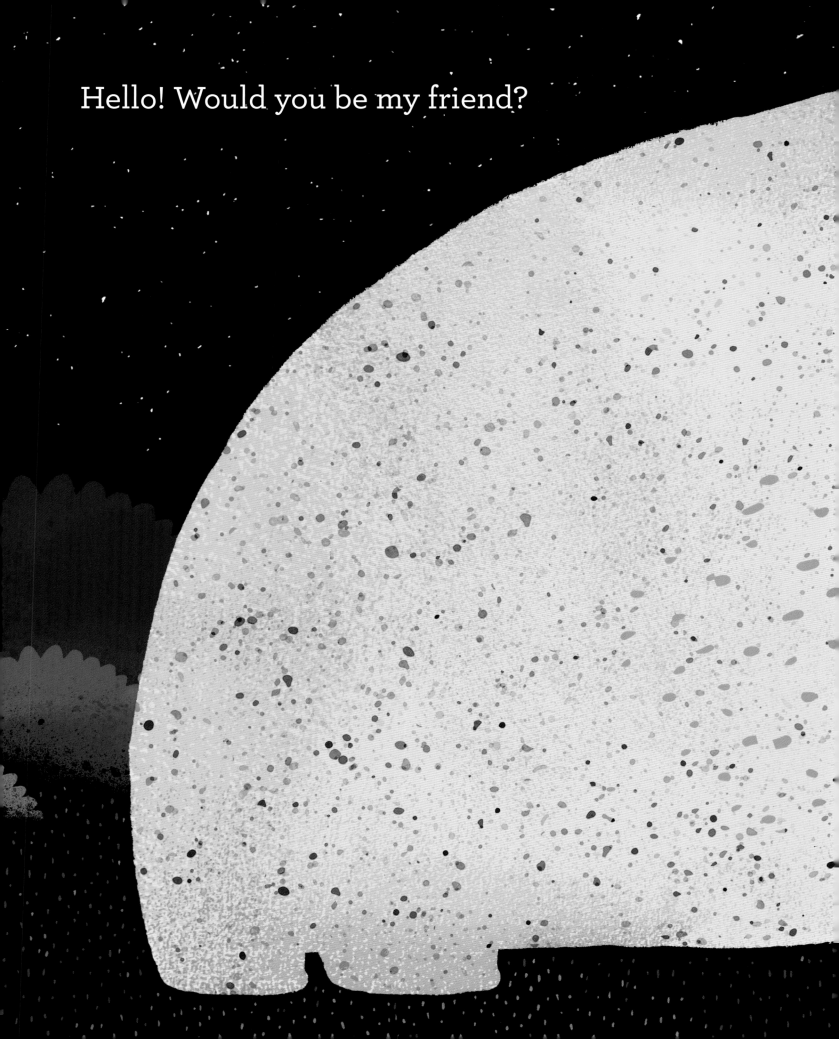

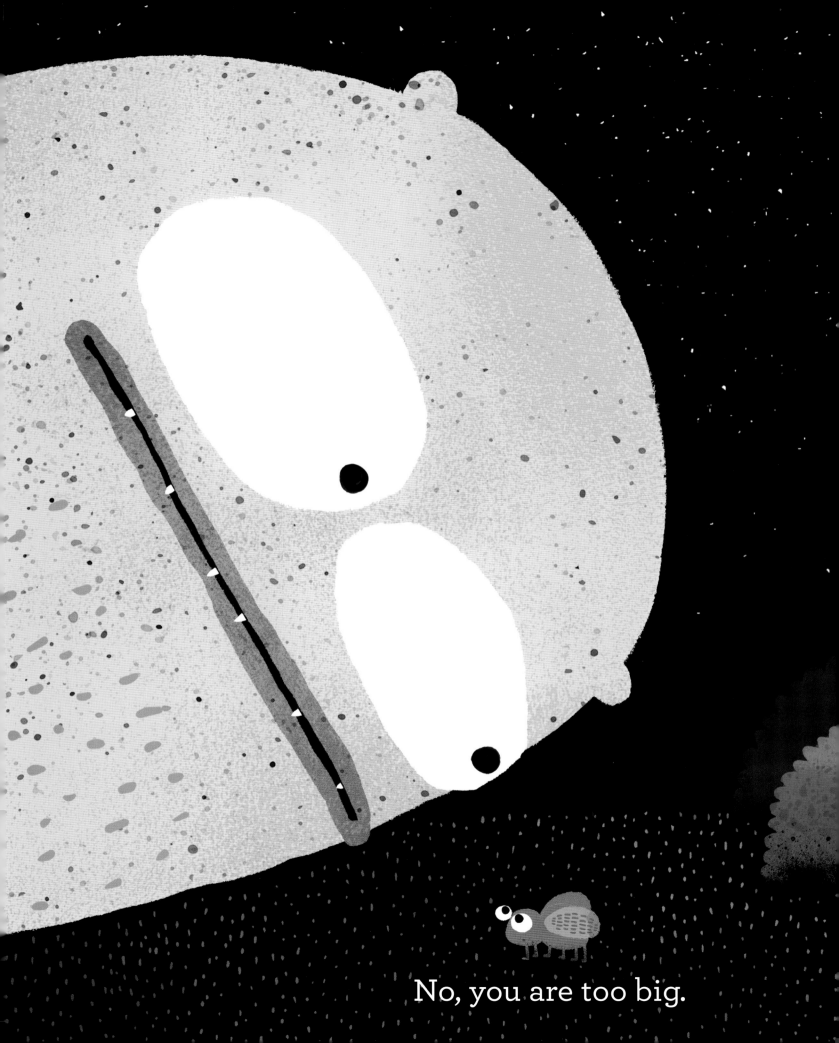

No, you are too big.

Hello! Would you be my friend?

No, you are too small.

Hello! Would you be my friend?

No, you are too scary.

Hello! Would you be my friend?

No, you are too slow.

Hello! Would you be my friend?

No.

Hello, would you be my...

Never mind.

Goodbye.

What if I never find another friend?

What if I ate my only friend?

I just ate my friend.

FOR
Seamus and Ava

First published by Allen & Unwin in 2017

Copyright © text & illustrations, Heidi McKinnon 2017

Allen & Unwin
83 Alexander Street
Crows Nest NSW 2065
Australia
T. (61 2) 8425 0100
info@allenandunwin.com
www.allenandunwin.com

A Cataloguing-in-Publication entry is available from the National Library of Australia
www.trove.nla.gov.au

ISBN 978 1 76029 434 2

For teaching resources, explore
www.allenandunwin.com/resources/for-teachers

Cover and text design by Heidi McKinnon

Printed by Hang Tai Printing Company Limited, China

10 9 8 7 6 5

www. heidimckinnon.com

A huge thanks to:
Sally Rippin, Susannah Chambers, Cam at dirtypuppet.com
and my incredible dad, Sandy McKinnon.